When the Spirit Moves Me

When the Spirit Moves Me

Examinations of Faith

JOHN ZEDOLIK

RESOURCE *Publications* • Eugene, Oregon

WHEN THE SPIRIT MOVES ME
Examinations of Faith

Copyright © 2021 John Zedolik. All rights reserved. Except for brief quotations in critical publications or reviews, no part of this book may be reproduced in any manner without prior written permission from the publisher. Write: Permissions, Wipf and Stock Publishers, 199 W. 8th Ave., Suite 3, Eugene, OR 97401.

Resource Publications
An Imprint of Wipf and Stock Publishers
199 W. 8th Ave., Suite 3
Eugene, OR 97401

www.wipfandstock.com

PAPERBACK ISBN: 978-1-6667-1685-6
HARDCOVER ISBN: 978-1-6667-1686-3
EBOOK ISBN: 978-1-6667-1687-0

07/19/21

Contents

Acknowledgments	vii
The Time of Half Light Again	1
Parallax	2
Sacred Idyll	3
If Rather, Perpendicular	4
Cast	5
Imitatio Christi	6
Up-Angling	7
Simple Want	8
Final Repossession	9
Nourishing Abstinence	10
High Time Off	11
Déjà Vu	12
Liminal Space, Far from Grace	13
Inspired Perspective	14
Dominvs Maris Alti	15
Polished to Perfection	16
Split Attentions	17
Got Yer Back	18
Essential Feast	20
Felt Charisma	22
Fair Credence	25
Ongoing Surprise	26
Safety Net	28
Via Antica, Via Praesens	29

CONTENTS

No Purchase	31
Nothing Lost	32
Annual Account	33
Kenosis	34
Superior Utility	36
Angle	37
Ichthys	39
Supine Imagination	41
Passion Plea	42
Contrasting Account	43
Weighty Concern	44
Harvest Numbers	45
Ur-Text	46
Providing Accompaniment	47
Heading	48
Seraphic Searching	49

Acknowledgments

"The Time of Half Light Again" and "Parallax," in *Time of Singing, A Journal of Christian Poetry*, Volume 43, Number 1, Conneaut Lake, PA (Spring 2016)

"Sacred Idyll," in *Ancient Paths Online* (June 2016)

"If Rather, Perpendicular," in *Time of Singing, A Journal of Christian Poetry*, Volume 43, Number 2, Conneaut Lake, PA (Summer 2016)

"*Imitatio Christi*" and "Up-Angling," in *The Penwood Review*, Los Alamitos, CA (Spring 2017)

"Nourishing Abstinence," in *Time of Singing, A Journal of Christian Poetry*, Volume 44, Number 2, Conneaut Lake, PA (Summer 2017)

"High Time Off," "Liminal Space, Far from Grace," "Felt Charisma" [revised version], "*Dominvs Maris Alti*," and "Angle," in *Studio: A Journal of Christians Writing*, Number 148, Albury, New South Wales, Australia (June 2020)

"Déjà Vu," in *Time of Singing, A Journal of Christian Poetry*, Volume 46, Number 1, Conneaut Lake, PA (Spring 2019)

"Inspired Perspective," in *The Penwood Review*, Los Alamitos, CA (Spring 2018)

"Split Attentions," in *:lexicon*, Duquesne University, Pittsburgh, PA (Fall 2018)

"Got Yer Back" and "Fair Credence," in *The Penwood Review*, Los Alamitos, CA (Fall 2019)

"Essential Feast," in *Commonweal*, Volume 146, Number 7, New York, NY (April 12th, 2019)

"Safety Net," in *Ancient Paths Online* (December 24th, 2020)

ACKNOWLEDGMENTS

"*Via Antica, Via Praesens*," in *Today's American Catholic, A Journal of inquiry, reflection and opinion*, Hamden, CT (April 2020)

"Nothing Lost," in *Time of Singing, A Journal of Christian Poetry*, Volume 48, Number 1, Conneaut Lake, PA (Spring 2021)

"Supine Imagination" and "Ongoing Surprise," in *Today's American Catholic, A Journal of inquiry, reflection and opinion*, Hamden, CT (June/July 2020)

"*Ichthys*," in *Ancient Paths Online* (February 27th, 2021)

The Time of Half Light Again

The light is partial on the early April afternoon,
as if waiting for clearance, as I imagined when a boy,
from God the Father, while Christ hung dead on the cross,

after I had seen one of those movies tracing his life
where the skies darkened well before sunset, and the centurion
said, "Truly, this man was the Son of God."

The sky looks the same on this Good Friday, lid descending
and closing to gray and who knows what end? But the spring will
draw more pure sun to our wobbling axis as it continues,

and the curtain in the temple tears again and will do so at this time
next year through all my next ones

and beyond, as the sky's half-light makes wholes
for every and all under it.

Parallax

In the womb of childhood
I watched
Max Von Sydow—I think—or was it Jeffrey Hunter
in *The Greatest Story Ever Told* (I think that was the title)

as Jesus

utter, near his ascension to certain heaven

"I shall be with you to the end of time."

taking this promise boy-earnestly
into cool sheets within night walls, in comfort,
beyond prime-time

And Jesus or Max or Jeffrey playing Jesus

with his all-piercing eyes, tenacious, inspiring trust

has left his mark—nay, deep incision—

that veins up from memory's mine
where resides the RCA set's dark-battling glow
to the sun and breath of today.

But is it Max or Jeffrey or Jesus
promising so much?

Sacred Idyll

At ease, Saint John on Patmos,
you certainly are, in Poussin's vision,
an old man past the struggle, alive

and reclining under light blue and
lighter clouds amid the ruins, soft
and convenient, as the old order died

to leave old John living in a ninth
decade, spared the fate of his mates,
thus relaxed and free to write his book

and ponder the result—win an amphora
of olive oil, if his time were previous—
ante Dominum—and he were battling

Sophocles on some hillside theater
stage—or better, Aristophanes, the comic—
but he's escaped and won. I leave him

with his *logos*, intent upon the Koine Greek.
He can ink without bother, Christ's favorite,
the holy leisure, I suppose, his reward.

If Rather, Perpendicular

If we imagined the divine as
horizontal instead of vertical,

would saints have wheels—or skis,
in northern reaches?

Would worshippers look into the
distance with leveled eyes and

imagine their loved ones beyond
the line of trees, hills, or concrete?

And would houses of worship be tunnels
whose ends projected their sacred symbol,

to the vanishing point where vision
failed and faith necessarily took over entirely,

in that realm of metaphor perpendicular
to ours and our privileging of up and those

wings awfully useful to reach it?

Cast

The eye of God splinters,
casts its gold flecks
like a million, million

far fish, from high and low
limbs, to scatter and sigh
in their fluttering school

over the flats and folds,
which receive them
with an answering click

sharp as November wind
or just silence in the end,
where the bits sleep

on the soil, waiting
to sink in winter then rise,
seeking the new sky

through root and bud
as the body of holy earth
grows, quick, again

Imitatio Christi

Could you be Christed,
cardinaled to the cosmos
by head, arms, and legs,

Longinused so bled
and drained of water
for the hard dry earth

below while they cast
for your garments as if
just linen or wool undyed

with regal purple of crushed
murex by the thousands
that yours are certainly not

and still on you anyway
as you imagine stretching
and dying, limbs limbering

to zenith, nadir, zephyr, and dawn
a poor clay cartoon, even
as your imagination plumbs

two thousand years and more
miles, a feat so light, the *crux vera*
it creates has no weight at all.

Up-Angling

I cast for God, a fish in the cloud sea,
and the line winds out, up, and out

until catching on a branch-end of wind.
I pull, feel the snag, yank back empty,

the hook polished to chalice silver
catching the sudden sun.

I take care not to take the prong
and barb in fingers then cast with easy flick,

hoping to receive in this try some greater
of what I have just given the deep water of sky.

Simple Want

I desire to be Raphael

rapha El

for who else is to do it?

And I would accept wings
in the deal, but that probably
is too much when I am returning
to whole.

Rapha El is enough for me.
I accept sound body and mind
sine forma angeli

and wait here intact until
the change to subtler skin

Final Repossession

License-holding angels must
have taken the canary-yellow car,
for space has opened to let

light on the asphalt long since
crumbling to dark gravel
that will absorb rain, sink

the ice without resistance
so yielding dandelions
and their eventual puffs

drifting off and away
to generate their kind again
in some lot of gray to black

vacated by a vehicle, repoed
by those working angels
without the need for stealth

or subterfuge, the owner having
left the deed in the glove compartment,
folded like those wings

when those permanent reclaimers
reach this particular, emptied earth

Nourishing Abstinence

Christ faces Satan in the desert,
his own demon, for forty days
of test and denial, kingdoms

and lust tossed aside,
but toiling in the struggle even
as Old Nick purrs like a cat

to probe his weakness heightened
by thirst and hunger, so one
might wonder if the Savior

flicked a horn of the tempter
just to show what a joker he was,
lightening his own mood,

perhaps thinking of cousin John's
grasshoppers and wild honey
(*if only I could have a bite!*)

and determining he was better
for the hunger, smooth and free
from the sticky-sweet and toothsome crunch

High Time Off

It looked like the bishop on a bicycle,
zipping down the trail at river's edge,
insouciant in spring T-shirt and shorts,

so perhaps he was ducking the duties
of Easter mass that might be onerous
to him after these many holy years.

And besides, it's time for his flock to start
fending for itself, facing the wolves.
Not forever will they be lambs of God,

so maybe the bishop should shirk
the bulk of his pastoral care, catch
the devil in his pedal's wake,

make Sunday safe for all believers
though they might be wondering
if their chief forgot the day and date.

Déjà Vu

Lazarus, losing his life at last,
years after the regaining,

might have gotten it into his head
to request of the Nazarene

another performance. Yet he might not
have been aware of the latter's

departure in fulfillment of an agreement,
so unavailable to raise the old man

who would just have to take this second,
final demise and the succeeding state,

worth the doubt, he might hope,
and the decades' wait

Liminal Space, Far from Grace

What passed in the gray slate seconds
as Judas dropped from oxygen—*spiritvs vitae*—
to not or worse when the rough rope

held only dead weight that must have swung
slightly in the Levantine breeze like a large
pendulum tolling the time that might have moved

unmeasured for Iscariot since the taking of silver—
the heft of thirty—and the giving over of his Christ,
but now steady and reliable until mere physics

intervened and stopped the swaying,
to leave a little less for the land and the living,
who would cut down the hunk with a well-used

fisherman's knife well beyond that sheet of iron
his mind had time to traverse, considering the exchange,
before the twisted fiber squeezed out even more than despair?

Inspired Perspective

Tow truck with a cruciform
attachment on its rear,
more than an afterthought—

a conjurer of *Corpus Christi*
to me as I observe from a modest
height that yields the effect

of epic cinema circa 1956
tracing the life of Him
from birth under the special star

to resurrection whose immediate
cause I perceive, as the suffering
shape appears in my spirited vision,

stretched upon the rust of the strong,
supporting steel yet soft enough
to carry the bleeding limbs

and crowning thorns to the red light,
with a pause then down the hill empty
of skulls, and out of my double-sight.

Dominvs Maris Alti

With every closing of the door,
the nailed-up crucifix clangs
On the ridges of blue plaster
the boy had imagined more often

as a sea reaching between the studs
to unfathomable horizontal depths
that the icon stretched to four points

under the bolted acronym INRI
must have calmed as he did Galilee,
much smaller than that fancied ocean

behind and under that finished room
sounding for miles more than thousands
and years the same, which echoed the words

of him reproduced stiff on the frame:

Svm alpha et omega

stretching even with its cheap-metal source
to the limits of the abyss

netting any fish and feeders lurking in razor tooth
within that depthless wall.

Polished to Perfection

God only knows what would have been,
so he must have a lidless eye
the size of a globe containing all,
transparent without reflection,

beyond whatever Windex insists
its recipe of ammonia and water
can do, since it always leaves streaks.
No, God's sphere would fool any bird

into a maiming crash if that sublunary
bunch of feathers and a beak could reach
that distant better-than-glassy curve,
but it's safe—far inside the diameter—

no danger of that arcing end—with us
who can only see as far as—until the
wee earth bends a bit too much for
peepers the size of plucked grapes.

Split Attentions

Playing bastard kin to minor chords
on an electric organ

—unoccupied kids in grandparents' house—

under a painting of Jesus praying,
lit by a dim, incandescent bulb

but we were not—as we pressed
various discordant combinations
of two neighboring keys,

fumbling for music that might
uncover easily, an Easter egg
to be found in shorn grass,

pink pastel, kid-friendly amid the green,

but Jesus, on his knees, looked up
and away toward his father's heaven,

his hands and attention too tightly
clasped to grant our unknowing plea

for sweet, saving melody.

Got Yer Back

Other: You know that guy?

Pete: Nah

Ah—the first, feels like a good punch, doesn't it?
—Right into that fool's gut—

Another: Come on, don't you know him?

Pete: No, I don't!

But now blasting these jerks is getting to be a pain, right?
—when you're minding your own business—

The Last: You do know him.

Pete: I said no!

Wow, these people just don't give up, do they?
—should just leave well enough alone—

The Rooster: Cock-a-doodle-doo!

[Pete hears the bird and turns
toward the receding prisoner
who is still within eyesight.]

Pete: (to himself) Ah, Christ! He was right? Goddam—me!

But he won't.

[Pete exits, damming up his tears.]

Essential Feast

Fish-fry every Friday night
during Lent at Saint John's
Saint Mary's Saint Michael's
and many, many more

—no meat for the faithful—

The hot oil must be sacred
chrism to cook that cod,
perch, or flounder to blessed
crispy crust while saving

the moist purity of its
innocent white flanks
the parishioner must partake

—not quite the Body of Christ—

but a cut above the accompanying
cole slaw, fries, and Sunday
to Thursday fare

(excluding the Host at morning mass)

leading the communicant to digestion
transcending the purely material

nourishing the hungry soul
long practiced in abstinence,
disciplined in this season
of forsaking the flesh.

Felt Charisma

i.

The Magdalene anoints your feet,
Christ, and mingles her hair's oil
with that in the vessel, so what honor

you must have felt—equal to hers—
as the proffered locks cleansed your flesh
as smoothly as salvation, smothering as soul

(*Accept this service, these threads of me.*)

she might say, silent in the act of ablution,
silk coils engaged, a deep cascade,
muscles intent on the ministering grace.

ii.

In Istanbul stands the hooped (lopped)
column of Constantine, Çemberlitaş,
in Turkish, at whose base

    (now muffled in stone of a millennium)

—legend has it—

rests the Magdalene's oil,

Christ's leftover loaves,
and Noah's ax.

So does that unction hold a trace of contact with Him—

atoms accreted with divinity's
extra-electromagnetic pull—

waiting for the stones to shear
and spill the vessel to the needy streets,
miles, and souls?

iii.

And if settled then buried
in Provence, long miles
from the Levantine launch,

does her dust and bone

> (the stain of the chrism
> her remains in earth retain)

communicate the touch,
the massaging of sacred skin
turned long since to spirit?

iv.

I sense the slippery stuff
slide through the ages,
a thick river, current complete

as flows those through
carven caves in ever night
of blind fish and crawlers

but channels unbroken,
no empty pockets sundering
self and many from source,

unseen, but too deep to erase

—ευ χαρις—

that course of good grace.

Fair Credence

Be not so hard upon Thomas,
for his doubt ensured humility,

thus his deeds would not be rash,
no impetus from certainty to reach

for a sword and sever yet another's ear.

Fingers into the nail holes
and Longinus's rib-thrust—

the empiricist needs the data
for proof before conclusion

and action—so this reasonable man
of measured faith. Cut him

some charitable slack—Didymus,
the twin—believer and skeptic—

spirit and flesh the necessities
to follow the further way.

Ongoing Surprise

I push the red button
to request the sign
allowing me to cross,

directing the motored
hulks to desist for seconds
from their determined journeys,

once—twice—thrice

though the first will suffice.
It must be a slight neurosis
that forces my hand to redundancy

as if the odds will be better
that the little strider in white lights
will offer me unchallenged passage

—not guaranteed but made more probable—

a gambler's choice,

sprung by my finger's repeated pressure

from the lack of trust I have invested
in the system and its promise of free
movement that leaves limbs whole—

The figure appears. The machinery
fulfills its end of the bargain.
I saunter across the intersection

    surprised that once again

I have doubted like Thomas
    and pressed three times into the metal's
    recess, no wound, just the reliability
    neither of the flesh

nor of the divine.

Safety Net

Snow on Christmas Eve is only
silent sugar-dust of grace, as light
and gentle as mother's lace,

no threat to life tires into hallowed
space and the bodies hurtling
in the same narrow trace,

even after *missi sumus* into the early
hours of the Natal Day, still dark,
well ahead of the Son's warming

Sol that will dispel any fear
of post-solstice slip that might crumple
and mar the Holy Day's cheer of each

humble crèche within its hoped-for
timbers and held fire that will keep
out the wind, night, and cold—

unwelcome and unauthorized
—flatly impermissible—upon this Eve
and Morn where a certain Star's

singe and shimmer guarantees
the rubber will embrace the road
between the candled church
and slumber in the safe abode.

Via Antica, Via Praesens

Quo Vadis?

I don't know; I missed the stop.

Just get off here, she kindly says,
three hundred yards or meters,

give or take a few umbrella pines
back to the correct prong to find

the honeycomb of the dead
carved beneath the soil and ancient street.

Then at the base of the trident's spread,
I stride without thought to a small church:

Quo Vadis

that remembers the plot where
Peter met Him and turned back around.

Quo Vadis?

He asked the man who must have forgotten
his thrice-denial before that cock,
long-dead even then, crowed—

—then remembered.

*

I took the Rock's planned way
then found my path down
into the tunneled, hollowed tufa—
hallowed (under) ground.

Quo Vadis?

I remember the question.
It accompanies me as I delve, still proceed.

No Purchase

The chartered bus lugged
the travelers within two hundred meters
of Vesuvius's mischievous caldera

above the sweating miles
of volcanic green bounty and tendrils
of rising road not felt in cushioned comfort

the trek on foot brief and mild to the lip
and a portion around, passing both ways
a modest shelter selling

sangre de Christo

wine for the memory
and an evening's uncoiling on the plain below

—but who deserved His Blood
after just a minutes' trot?

Better left to those few who might
trudge up the twists of the mount

—*Via Arduosa*—

A reward for the push and pain of the entire ascent.

Nothing Lost

Did the paste Christ made of mud
and saliva to open the eyes

of the blind man smell sour
and earthy to one whose remaining

senses must have been heightened
by the loss of one? And did he leave

the mixture to run a bit then crust,
flake off in a warm breeze, returning

to dust and water vapor whence
the elemental matter arose,

the stuff of continents and oceans.
But went—where—the shiver of grace?

Perhaps it webbed without a sight
or sound into wings later to descend

to the twelve in a cycle of charisma
so not lose a molecule or drop, loop

heavenward then down to those
in deserts thirsting for sight.

Annual Account

There is / there was
no year one (*anno domini* for some)

so zero is / has been swallowed
into less than nothing

where hide the disallowed
of humanity's contrivance

to welter in these questions
of those who ask, certainly

few, given the billions who give
no thought to the missing

cycle that cannot be missed
since it does not exist

except in those minds that wonder
what living for 365 days

in an arc of time that does not count
and consider that Christ—

arrived under the star—the cause of the shift
and non-being—could make up the amount.

Kenosis

Down, down to low earth,
skin and clunking bone,

wings off to ape-kin arms
to be stretched to sag

'til tension dies in death
and sacrifice for the beasts,

how heavy must the body
be, held up by iron and beam

against mundane gravity,
it will take three days

just to rise in this assumed
meat and walk for nearly

six weeks against the hard-packed
and grasping ground that must

finally relax its reaching claws,
steady nails and depth-grip

as the base material, rind
to pit, flakes to fluff and less

on the wind while he ascends
to ether, dross sloughed off,

heft now unnecessary, the burden
borne, the ages will keep the weight.

Superior Utility

Muslims hold that God
transformed Abraham's pyre
to water and the hot coals to fish

—if one sees a white one,
heaven's door will open—

what a better use than
burning bones to sour ash

and singeing the semi-desert
with wood flamed to the unforgiving

parch of lethal orange-red, instead
a cool pool in which to bathe and drink,

copious carp upon which to dine,
need met—when it is no longer necessary

to send off a sacred body already on its way

—Now look for the flash like foam,
in the ripples, the fins of holy lottery,

stirring the air to a charitable breeze,
swinging the hinges for the fortunate eye.

Angle

Dismas soon-to-be-saint, crucified
upon Christ's right side,

which Orthodox crosses indicate
with their short transverse

near the base rising to the repentant
unseen, since taken

as Christ had promised—opposite
the damned Gestas, selfish

and sliding down like a player
of chutes (snakes)

and ladders on the low side
of that foot-and-nail rest

that one might imagine a scale
in reverse, the weighted

down in adamant sin the lesser
worth, as gold and its hard

desire are as granite, lead,
and anchor chains

to the Redeemer who takes
through the gates

even those tonned with wrong
and error who seek

to be shriven so washed
as light as

cast feathers, motes, and dandelion seeds.

Ichthys

Pontius's hands,
which he dipped
in the basin's water

must have been pale
as the ivory of Pheidias's
Zeus in its dim temple-box,

veinless like an languid
limb of Aphrodite lost
in an Aegean wreck—

so fish swimming for a moment
to splash in the shallow bronze
that would not reflect his face,

for otherwise he might have
known himself, as Apollo's oracle
at Delphi advised, pagan-wise,

seen his sallow fins, flabby
in the flash of liquid habitat,
that does not admit a rigid

row of bones necessary
to make the straight decision
and determined trace

on the dry land sometimes parched,
without spirit or rain,
to unforgiving rock, adamant terrain.

Supine Imagination

Renovation had exposed some
apparent joists below an arc
of floor in San Stefano in Rotondo,

so I might lie down on them
in mortification as witness
to Saint Lawrence grilled

upon a gridiron as depicted
in one of the encircling murals
Charles Dickens found so disturbing,

though only sustain a few splinters
and a pain in the scapulae, stiff
muscles if my stay were of any

duration beyond innocuous seconds,
so a pale *imitatio sancti* not even
worthy of the impersonation,

just an indulgence of my moment
within the sacred circle, which would
not buy me out of purgation

more quickly, just let me feel
the martyred hero, feeling no
heat, not much pain at all.

Passion Plea

God-man nailed to a tree
in turn nailed to another tree,
large and still flowing sap,

left beside the site of self-
immolation now only
a hollow on the hillside

where the house had stood
until the ignition in dying
summer's lingering twilight,

no Good Friday but a Saturday
un-sanct so like the rest
for most others and the trunk

thus unmarked until some
unknown later day when Christ's
image in his sacrifice would preside

under the limbs that overlooked
the bulldozed hole. The supplicant
holding the hammer and its force

hoping mercy on the hill un-Golgotha
for he who created the burst and fire,
a thoroughly reasonable Christian desire.

Contrasting Account

According to Acts,
The Iscariot fell,
bursting out his viscera
upon his purchased ground

deemed Akeldama, Field of Blood,[1]

because with that bought—
so not a suicide wrought,

but the acid fruits of gut-busting despair
impossible to bury so must find the air,

a fate much worse than hanging
self-strung from a redbud bough?[2]

But, if unwilled, then might the gentle
hand of high mercy, descending, allow?

1. found in *Wikipedia*. Accessed 17 May 2020
2. found in *Wikipedia*. Accessed 17 May 2020

Weighty Concern

Tu qui peccata mundi tollis,
take these sins from my shoulders,

for I am unequal to the daily task,
these weights, acute-angled boulders

pushing my clay feet into the ground
of low matter that gives too much,

and imagine the throng, the billions,
who need the lift of your light touch.

Harvest Numbers

Whither the scraps of those
five barley loaves that fed
the five thousand souls?

Apparently gathered
in a wicker basket to feed
another five grand and possibly

a few triple-zero counts more as
the mathematical morphs
to elliptical and numbers

no longer add up but run
round to repeat fifty times
ten times ten and so around

again to the sum of satiety
that the Son has ordained
for these fishermen's fares

and their—and our—daily bread.

Ur-Text

In the beginning was the Word,
so I come back to the base of reason

as the ink to the clean white sheet
open to the infinite even as John

returns to John and his stated
source whence springs all's

inspiration—*a breathing in*—
of the conscious seed that sprouts

stalks up to the air and roots down
through the soil, which quicken

and bind every atom, mote into
a seamless One, sprung from first

Logic whose gray premises and proofs
will burst in gold, blue, and green.

Providing Accompaniment[3]

Shadrach, Meshach,
and Abednego remained

cool flesh in the fiery furnace,
seen by the minions of the king

accompanied by a fourth who,
they uttered, must be a son

of God, providing relief
and a spur to song from cool

throats and lungs, so heard
from without, no dross dripping

down into rivulets and away
from the desired ore but flying

up and out on grace's wing,
honey melody in the ears

echoing yet with ice-chill *thring*
that we may hear even under

heavy heat that despots direct
but which our best angel will always deflect.

3. from Daniel 3

Heading

Winter has stripped
the honeysuckles down
to frames that writhe

like Christ-crown of thorns
above the cracked street,
but no blood-coursed face

below nor strained, savaged
limbs, only ghosts, gray winds
rattling through and down the turn

to the ramps conducting
the cars into the flow, too fast
and curving to suffer concern.

Seraphic Searching

Are six wings enough
for the hexapterygon,

who must fly to God's
sun so might require

a pair threefold to withstand
the height and generate

the lift needed for such
a feat, and if one pinion
of the six is fixed with wax,

which melts in the heat,
so producing the possibility
of plunge into unkind seas

that might soak the wing
and swallow the messenger,
drown any message divine-sent,

so five more, sufficiently
engineered redundancy, to stave
off the pull of creatured earth,

a place for mortal plodding lead
and only a single set of feathers
for those designed, destined

to fly, who only seek the embrace
of atmosphere whose arms are thin
and heaven's route cannot trace?

www.ingramcontent.com/pod-product-compliance
Lightning Source LLC
Chambersburg PA
CBHW072035060426
42449CB00010BA/2263